Park

Katie Dicker

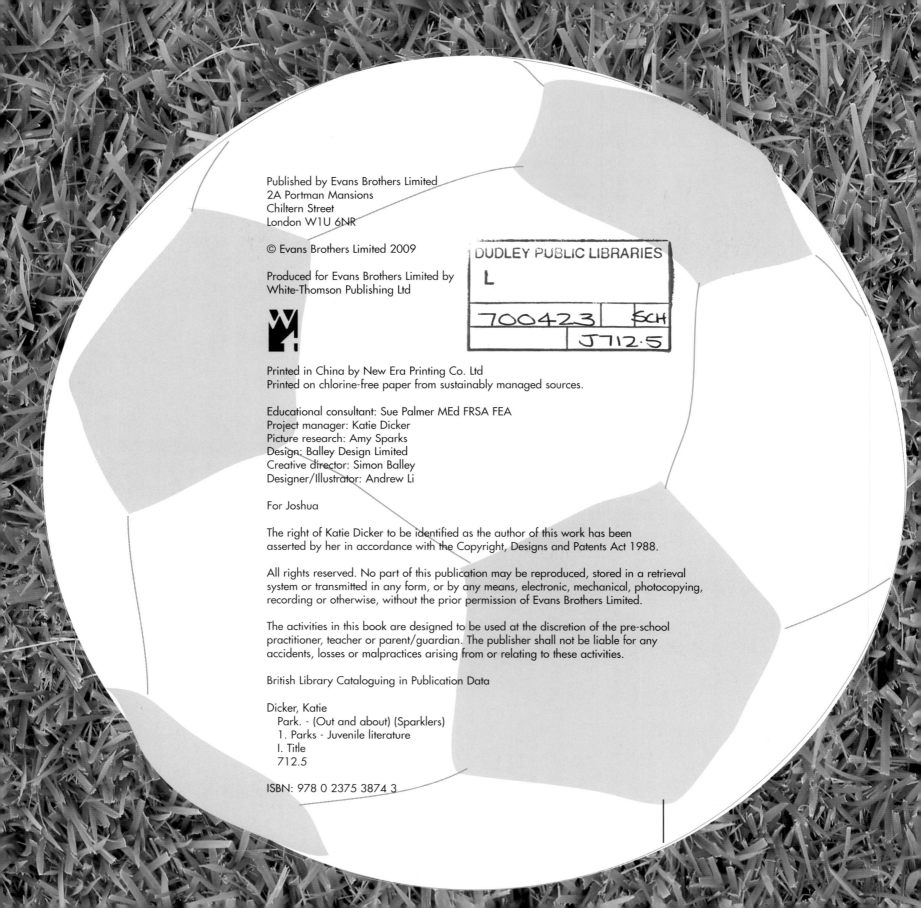

Published by Evans Brothers Limited
2A Portman Mansions
Chiltern Street
London W1U 6NR

© Evans Brothers Limited 2009

Produced for Evans Brothers Limited by
White-Thomson Publishing Ltd

Printed in China by New Era Printing Co. Ltd
Printed on chlorine-free paper from sustainably managed sources.

Educational consultant: Sue Palmer MEd FRSA FEA
Project manager: Katie Dicker
Picture research: Amy Sparks
Design: Balley Design Limited
Creative director: Simon Balley
Designer/Illustrator: Andrew Li

For Joshua

British Library Cataloguing in Publication Data

Dicker, Katie
    Park. - (Out and about) (Sparklers)
    1. Parks - Juvenile literature
    I. Title
    712.5

ISBN: 978 0 2375 3874 3

Contents

Park time

Come and play in the park!

How high can YOU jump?

skip!

5

On the grass

springy!

The grass is soft to lie on.

Follow the path

spring blossom

Flat paths are good for cycling.

This footpath is covered
with autumn leaves.

9

Trees and leaves

How wide is the tree trunk?

vein

What's the LARGEST leaf you can find?

11

By the lake

How far can YOUR boat sail?

ripple

Walk the dog

Woof!

Harvey loves to go to the park.

14

Footprints

Can you find the animals' footprints?

What marks do
YOU leave behind?

crunch

17

Picnic time

Yum!

What picnic food do YOU like to eat?

At the playground

Hi!

The playground is full of new friends to meet.

20

Sparklers books are designed to support and extend the learning of young children. The **Food We Eat** titles won a Practical Pre-School Silver Award and the **Body Moves** titles won a Practical Pre-School Gold Award. The books' high-interest subjects link in to the Early Years curriculum and beyond. Find out more about Early Years and reading with children from the National Literacy Trust (www.literacytrust.org.uk).

Themed titles
Park is one of four **Out and About** titles that encourage children to explore outdoor spaces.
The other titles are:
Garden   Seaside   Wood

A CD to accompany the series (available from Evans Publishing Group tel 020 7487 0920 or email sales@evansbrothers.co.uk) provides sound effects from each environment, as well as popular songs and rhymes that relate to outdoor exploration.

Areas of learning
Each **Out and About** title helps to support the following Foundation Stage areas of learning:
Personal, Social and Emotional Development
Communication, Language and Literacy
Mathematical Development
Knowledge and Understanding of the World
Physical Development
Creative Development

Making the most of reading time
When reading with younger children, take time to explore the pictures together. Ask children to find, identify, count or describe different objects. Point out colours and textures. Allow quiet spaces in your reading so that children can ask questions or repeat your words. Try pausing mid-sentence so that children can predict the next word. This sort of participation develops early reading skills.

Follow the words with your finger as you read. The main text is in Infant Sassoon, a clear, friendly font designed for children learning to read and write. The labels and sound effects add fun and give the opportunity to distinguish between levels of communication. Where appropriate, labels, sound effects or main text may be presented phonically. Encourage children to imitate the sounds.

As you read the book, you can also take the opportunity to talk about the book itself with appropriate vocabulary such as "page", "cover", "back", "front", "photograph", "label" and "page number".

You can also extend children's learning by using the books as a springboard for discussion and further activities. There are a few suggestions on the facing page.

Pages 4–5: Park time

Draw a large park scene or cut out a photograph from a magazine. Make a collection of labels with park words and encourage children to help you to stick them to the appropriate parts of the picture – such as grass, path, trees, playground, bench, lake, litter bin. Talk to children about the expanse and variety of a park area and the different types of games that can be played there.

Pages 6–7: On the grass

Children may enjoy sitting or lying on an expanse of dry grass. Encourage them to describe what it feels and smells like. Help a group of children to make patterns of their own on the grass, such as making flower shapes or forming shadows in the sunlight.

Pages 8–9: Follow the path

Draw a simple maze and encourage children to follow the paths to get to the fountain (or treasure!). Talk to children about good reasons to stick to the paths in a park (to avoid muddy grass and to keep off flowerbeds, for example) and why paths are good for activities on wheels. Encourage children to be aware of the needs of other park users when they explore a park for themselves.

Pages 10–11: Trees and leaves

Collect a selection of leaves from a local park and encourage children to group them in order of size. Use books or the Internet to help the children identify which trees they are from. Encourage children to compare and contrast the different leaves. What colour are they? What do they feel like?

Pages 12–13: By the lake

Help children to make their own boat or raft made from paper or twigs. Sail the boats on a nearby pond or a large pool of water. Which model boats are the best at sailing and why? How are they affected by the weather conditions? Children may also enjoy trying to stand on one leg like a duck.

Pages 14–15: Walk the dog

Children may enjoy making their own sausage dog with modelling balloons. See for example, http://www.cheekotheclown.co.uk/balloons.htm for ideas. Encourage children to find pictures of different types of dogs using books, magazines or the Internet to help them to become more familiar with dogs they may meet in a park.

Pages 16–17: Footprints

Children may enjoy making their own footprints on paper using non-toxic craft paints. Make a collage of the footprints on the wall. Who has the largest footprint? Who has the smallest?

Pages 18–19: Picnic time

Encourage children to think of a menu for a park picnic. Talk to children about the importance of a balanced diet and what makes good picnic food. Children may enjoy having an indoor mini picnic of their own, sitting on a blanket and sharing pieces of fruit, for example.

Pages 20–21: At the playground

Draw an outline of a park playground and encourage children to colour in the different rides. Which rides are their favourite? Talk to children about using the playground safely and helping to keep it a pleasant place for other children, by putting litter in the bin for example. Children may enjoy designing a poster about keeping a park clean and tidy.

Index

Picture acknowledgements:
Alamy: 12 (Glenn Harper), 15 (Andrew Linscott); **Corbis:** cover boy (Moodboard), 4 (Randy Faris), 5 (AKIRA/amanaimages), 6 (Simon Jarratt), 11 (image100), 14 (Ron Chapple), 17 (KAZUO OGAWA/amanaimages); **Getty Images:** 7 (Martin Barraud), 9 (Andrew Olney), 10 (Steven Puetzer); **IStockphoto:** cover grass, cover sky (JLFCapture), 8 (Hans F. Meier), 20 (Thomas Perkins); **Photolibrary:** 19 (Robert Llewellyn); **Shutterstock:** cover swing, cover tree (Jan Martin Will), 2–3 grass (Smit), 13 (Sonya Etchison), 16 duck (Goran Kuzmanovski), 16 dog (Ferenc Szelepcsenyi), 16 squirrel (Eric Isselée), 16 pigeon (innocent), 16 footprints (Bill Heller), 18 (iofoto), 21 (Rossario), 22–23 grass (Smit), 24 grass (Smit).